The Bayer Color Atlas of
Hypertension

Volume 3

The Bayer Color Atlas of
Hypertension

Volume 3

Peter F. Semple
The Medical Research Council Blood Pressure Unit
Western Infirmary, Glasgow

and

George B. M. Lindop
University Department of Pathology
Western Infirmary, Glasgow

**Pharmaceutical
Division**

Pharmaceutical Division

Bayer Corporation
400 Morgan Lane
West Haven, CT 06516-4175

Dear Doctor:

Volume III of the new *Bayer Color Atlas of Hypertension* by Drs. Semple and Lindop of the University of Glasgow completes this valuable diagnostic aid provided to you by the Bayer Corporation, Pharmaceutical Division.

In this third and final text, investigations in pheochromocytoma, miscellaneous facts and other risk factors are the primary foci, and more than thirty-five beautiful photographs and illustrations are featured. As with Volumes I and II, the information contained in Volume III can be a valuable adjunct to your diagnostic and therapeutic skills.

We hope you find this series of value to your reference collection, and would be interested in learning your opinion on this work.

Sincerely,

H. Brian Allen, MD, FFPM
Director, Scientific Relations
and Health Care Communications

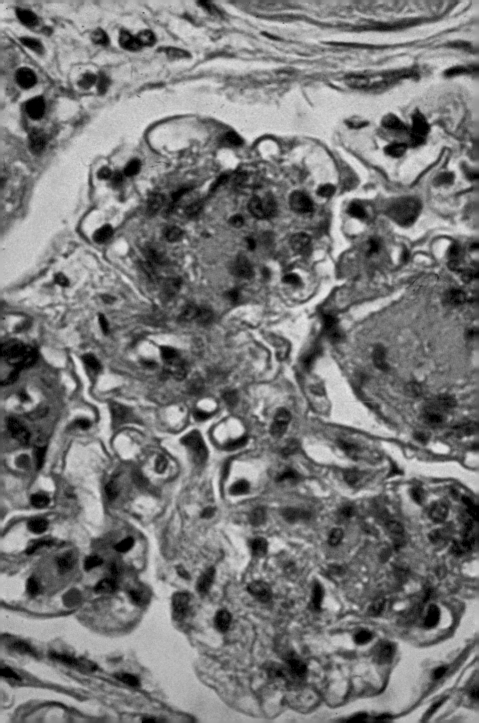

Contents

Investigation of secondary hypertension

Pheochromocytoma

Pheochromocytoma is a rare but well recognized form of secondary hypertension, which often causes problems in diagnosis. Routine screening for the condition in mild-to-moderate hypertension is not merited. Symptoms of pheochromocytoma include paroxysmal headache, sweating and pallor, or there may be paradoxical hypertension if treatment is given with a non-selective β-blocker. Interaction of circulating catecholamines with vasodilator vascular β_2 receptors normally offsets α-mediated vasoconstriction, so that blockade of the β_2 receptors alone prevents this modulation. Pheochromocytoma is often called the disease of 10 per cents: 10% are malignant, 10% bilateral and 10% extra-adrenal. Bilateral disease usually represents multiple endocrine neoplasia type 2a, which is inherited as a Mendelian dominant and associated with medullary carcinoma of the thyroid, a tumor arising in the calcitonin-secreting parafollicular cells. A less common variant is multiple neoplasia type 2b, which is associated with mucosal neuromata and skeletal deformities. In these inherited conditions, family screening is then necessary, using measurements of calcitonin and catecholamines. In some kindreds, genetic screening with DNA probes can now identify carriers with a high degree of confidence.

Diagnosis of pheochromocytoma is best established by measurement of plasma or urine concentrations of nor-adrenaline and adrenaline, although measurements of urine normetadrenaline or 4-hydroxy-3-methoxymandelic acid (HMMA) excretion may still have a place as screening procedures. Plasma levels of catecholamines are almost invariably raised if hypertension is present when samples are taken. Suppression tests with clonidine or pentolinium have particular value in distinguishing raised levels of plasma catecholamines, due to sympatho-adrenal activation caused by anxiety or heart failure from raised levels caused by pheochromocytoma. Most centers now prefer a test based on clonidine followed by measurements of plasma or urine levels of noradrenaline and adrenaline: overspill or neuronal catecholamine is abolished by α_2-mediated central inhibition of sympathetic nerve discharge. Plasma levels of chromogranin A or neuropeptide Y, present in catecholamine storage vesicles, may also be raised in pheochromocytoma but do not have a central role in diagnosis.

Most tumors can be localized by computed tomography but ultrasonographic scanning is sometimes useful. Ultrasound may not be sensitive enough to detect small tumors. In cases of difficulty, catheterization and selective sampling from the inferior vena cava and left renal vein can localize tumor tissue. Arteriography is less often performed, except to define tumor blood supply before definitive surgery in some instances. About 80% of pheochromocytomas take up met-iodobenzylguanidine (MIBG) and this chemical, labelled with ^{131}I, may be useful in scintigraphic localization of primary tumors and detection of metastatic deposits. Malignant tumours often metastasize to bone and isotope bone scanning with an agent such as ^{99}Tc-labelled diphosphonate is a useful preoperative procedure. Malignant tumors have sometimes been treated with therapeutic doses of [^{131}I]MIBG and some less differentiated tumors have shown a useful response to cytotoxic drug treatment.

The long-acting non-competitive α-blocker phenoxybenzamine remains the drug of choice for controlling arterial pressure in pheochromocytoma before operation: competitive drugs such as prazosin and labetalol have been somewhat disappointing in clinical practice. β_1-adrenergic blockers may be added to control cardiac rate. The preferred drug for intraoperative control of blood pressure is sodium nitroprusside. Nitroprusside has tended to supersede the competitive blocker phentolamine, which has rather transient effects on pressure, giving erratic control of pressure during tumor manipulation. Cardiac arrhythmias are generally prevented if control of pressure is maintained, although injected β-blockers may be a useful adjunct.

Miscellaneous
Hyperparathyroidism
There is an increased prevalence of hypertension in patients with primary hyperparathyroidism. Between 30 and 50% of affected patients have mild or moderately raised arterial pressure and some have left ventricular hypertrophy. The mechanism of the hypertension is not well understood but is probably related to the combined effects of extracellular hypercalcemia and excess parathyroid hormone. High blood pressure is not always corrected by surgery, which may reflect an overlap with primary hypertension. In primary hypertension, a proportion of patients show mild hypercalciuria and slightly raised levels of parathyroid hormone compared to controls with normal blood pressure. This may account for the increased incidence of renal calculus disease in patients with primary hypertension.

Acromegaly

Acromegaly is associated with hypertension and there is evidence that hypertension is related to increased body sodium content. Structural changes in cardiac and vascular muscle may also be relevant and the raised blood pressure does not always respond to normalization of plasma growth hormone levels.

Gestational hypertension

High blood pressure during pregnancy presents different problems. In normal pregnancy, blood pressure falls during the first trimester and may conceal pre-existing mild primary hypertension. There is also the syndrome of pre-eclamptic toxemia where hypertension with edema and proteinuria develops in late pregnancy associated with retardation of fetal growth. Thrombocytopenia and raised plasma concentration of urate are characteristic and intravascular volume is probably reduced. High blood pressure responds to antihypertensive drug treatment, but it is much less clear that such treatment retards the progress of the condition or produces any amelioration of the adverse effects on fetal growth and survival. Progress to eclampsia may, however, be prevented. The blood pressures rapidly return to normal levels after delivery but occasional instances of hypertension which persists for some days have been encountered.

Clear separation of this pre-eclampsia syndrome from primary hypertension in pregnancy is not always possible and patients with primary hypertension may also show retardation of fetal development *in utero*. Methyldopa is the drug that is currently preferred for control of pressure in pregnancy but this also reflects some lack of experience with other agents.

Estrogens and oral contraceptives The commonly used estrogen-containing oral contraceptives (containing $30\,\mu g$ of estrogen) have mild pressor effects in many women, so that monitoring of blood pressure before and after prescription is usual. A few individuals show a marked pressor response and these are often patients who go on to develop raised blood pressure in later life. Progestogen-only pills do not seem to raise blood pressure and may be prescribed in hypertension. Low-dose estrogen treatment given to women after ovarian estrogen secretion has ceased at the menopause does not seem to raise blood pressure, but the possibility that higher doses could have pressor effects in this age group should still be considered.

Coarctation of the aorta

Aorctic coarctation is a rare cause of hypertension which accounts for about 5–10% of all congenital cardiovascular anomalies. The lesion is relatively common in girls with XO gonadal dysgenesis or Turner's syndrome. Aorctic dissection, cerebral hemorrhage and heart failure are complications. High blood pressure occurs in the upper part of the body in vessels proximal to the coarctation, which is commonly situated at or just beyond the insertion of the ligamentum arteriosum. There are much lower blood pressures in the legs and this can be determined using a thigh cuff. Coarctation is usually suspected when the femoral and other leg pulses are found to be absent, much reduced or delayed compared to pulses in the arms. A mid-systolic murmur may be heard over the upper anterior chest and back but aortic systolic murmurs may originate in a bicuspid or stenotic aortic valve. Enlarged intercostal collateral vessels may be palpable around the chest with overlying vascular bruits.

Occasionally, the condition occurs at other sites such as the abdominal aorta and is then often associated with other congenital defects. The cause of hypertension in coarctation has not been well defined and initially a mechanical cause seems most likely. Most affected individuals are detected in the first year of life. Delayed surgical correction of coarctation leads to residual hypertension in 30–50% of patients, who may then require life-long drug treatment.

Other risk factors

Patients with raised blood pressure quite often have several other risk factors for atherosclerotic arterial disease. Epidemiological studies have shown that these factors tend to cluster together so that high blood pressure is then associated with high plasma levels of cholesterol, obesity and abnormal glucose tolerance. Intervention trials with antihypertensive drugs have shown at best that the risk of coronary events is reduced by only a third to a half of that expected. This may reflect the relatively short duration of these large trials set against the long duration of the process of atherogenesis.

Cigarette smoking remains the major and most easily altered risk factor for coronary heart disease. This is not related to chronic effects on blood pressure since population surveys have shown that smoking is either unrelated or inversely related to blood pressure. It has been estimated that about 30% of all coronary deaths are probably caused by smoking. In the Medical Research Council mild hypertension trial, the coronary event rate in male smokers was about twice the rate in non-smokers regardless of treatment and the difference was even sharper in women. In outcome trials, the difference in event rates between smokers with mild hypertension and non-smokers was often greater than the difference between active treatment and placebo. Smoking is strongly predictive of myocardial infarction and sudden death but less predictive of angina. Despite the absence of any correlation between smoking and blood pressure in population studies, an association between malignant hypertension and cigarette smoking has been observed and may be explained by the development of atherosclerotic renal artery stenosis in a small proportion of smokers. Patients with raised blood pressure who smoke cigarettes need every encouragement to quit.

Obesity and abnormalities in glucose and insulin metabolism are so frequent in hypertension that a common pathogenetic mechanism has been suspected. Insulin resistance and glucose intolerance which is independent of obesity are also more common in individuals with high blood pressure. An understanding of the increased risk of diabetes mellitus may be relevant to choice of drug for lowering pressure and is a further reason for encouraging obese patients with hypertension to lose weight. Obesity also has effects on left ventricular mass that are independent of arterial pressure. This may be important in the light of evidence that links left ventricular hypertrophy with arrhythmias and sudden death in hypertensive patients.

In individual patients with high blood pressure, a positive family history of coronary artery disease is a particularly strong pointer to the need to appraise other risk factors. Framingham and other prospective surveys in the West have shown that the risk of cardiovascular disease for a middle-aged man over a period of about 10 years shows a 10-fold gradient between those in the lowest quintile of the distribution of plasma cholesterol to those in the highest quintile. The sevenfold difference in death rate from ischemic heart disease between Japan and Scotland seems to be related to major differences in average cholesterol levels since hypertension and cigarette smoking are relatively common in both populations. Compared to total cholesterol levels, the low density lipoprotein (LDL) subfraction more closely predicts disease than total cholesterol and prediction is refined if the ratio of LDL to high density lipoprotein (HDL) cholesterol is used. HDL cholesterol seems to have some protective effect. The role of high triglyceride levels as an independent risk factor is debated but becoming more widely accepted. Measurement and treatment of raised levels of cholesterol and LDL cholesterol with diet, or drugs where appropriate, are central to the multiple risk factor approach increasingly used to treat the individual with high blood pressure. Effects on lipids may also be a consideration in selecting an antihypertensive drug for the hyperlipidemia patient although there are, as yet, no outcome trials that validate this approach.

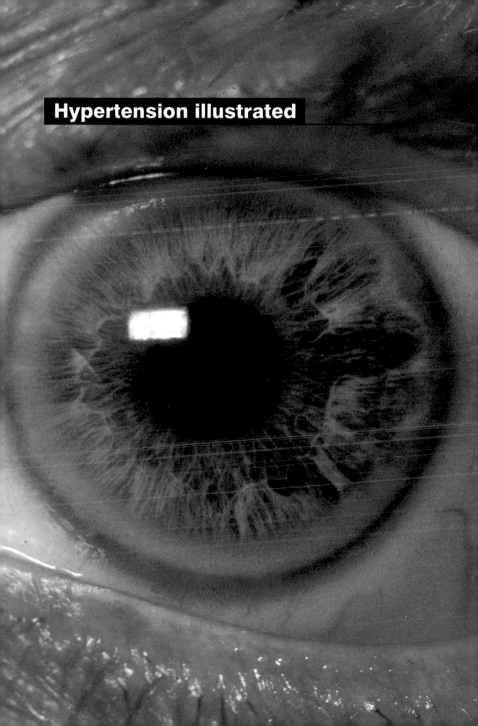

Hypertension illustrated

List of illustrations

Figure 1 Autosomal dominant polycystic kidney disease. Longitudinal ultrasound image of an enlarged and cystic right kidney. There is a low likelihood of the condition if an ultrasound study is negative in early adult life. In the commonest form, now designated PKDl, the genetic abnormality has been localized to the short arm of chromosome 16

Figure 2 Subarachnoid hemorrhage is usually caused by rupture of a berry aneurysm: berry aneurysms are associated with adult polycystic kidney disease. This reinforces the need for early detection and treatment of raised blood pressure in affected individuals

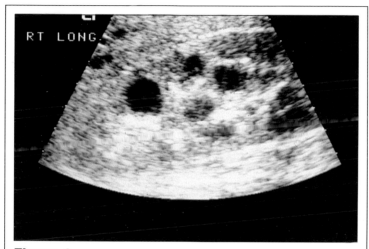

Figure 1

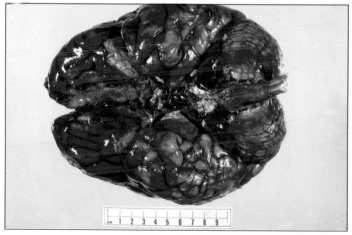

Figure 2

Figure 3 The kidney in adult polycystic kidney disease has been replaced by large cysts

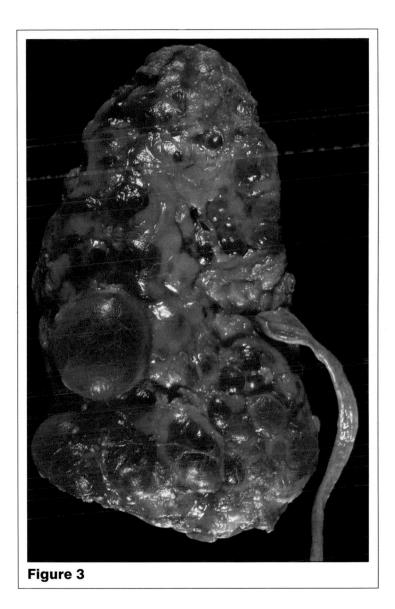

Figure 3

Figure 4 Micturating cystogram in an infant with severe vesico-ureteric reflux. Intrarenal reflux is seen at the upper poles. The other panel shows one of the dilated calyces with loss of overlying parenchyma

Figure 5 A rare cause of hypertension and hypokalemia is primary reninism. The small defect in the nephrogram phase of this arteriogram was shown to be a benign renin-secreting tumor of juxtaglomerular cells

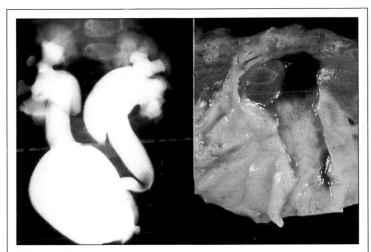

Figure 4

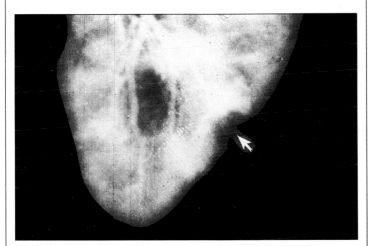

Figure 5

Figure 6 A low-power photomicrograph of the same juxtaglomerular cell tumor as in Figure 5. The immunoperoxidase stain with a renin antiserum (brown) confirms that cells contain renin. These tumors also contain tubular elements. There was diminished staining for renin in the adjacent cortex

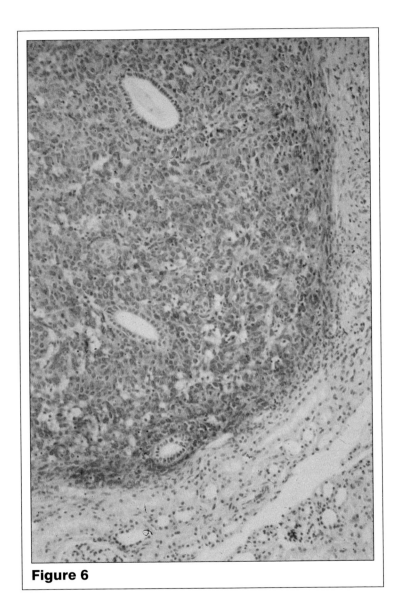

Figure 6

Figure 7 The electron microscopic appearance of a juxtaglomerular tumor cell. In the upper panel, dark-staining renin granules are evident. The dilated spaces are rough endoplasmic reticulum and a prominent Golgi apparatus can be seen. These are features of cells in an active phase of synthesis and secretion. In the lower panel is a typical paracrystalline renin 'protogranule' in the Golgi apparatus

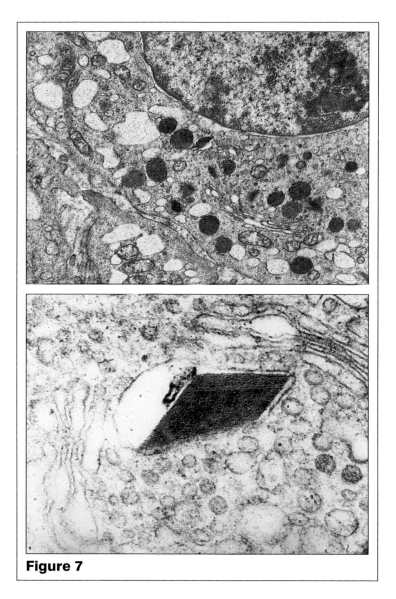

Figure 7

Figure 8 Micturating cystogram from a 13-year-old girl with malignant hypertension, showing reflux nephropathy with marked calyceal clubbing. The right kidney was shrunken and non-functioning. Reflux nephropathy is a common cause of hypertension in childhood and in young women with severe hypertension

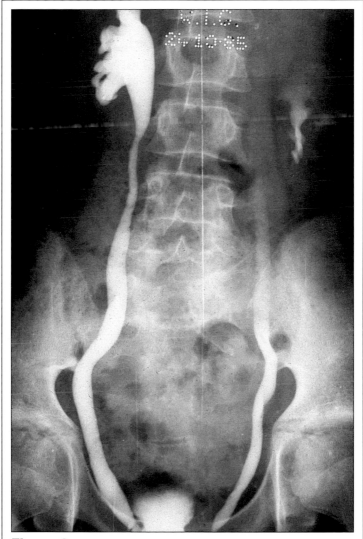

Figure 8

Figure 9 Computed tomography of the adrenals showing bilateral tumors in a 40-year-old man with primary aldosteronism. Such a finding is very unusual since aldosteronomas are almost invariably *unilateral*. In this case aldosterone secretion was confined to the smaller lesion on the left. This was demonstrated by measurements of aldosterone levels in adrenal venous blood. The larger right-sided lesion with the slightly lower attenuation coefficient was a non-functioning adenoma

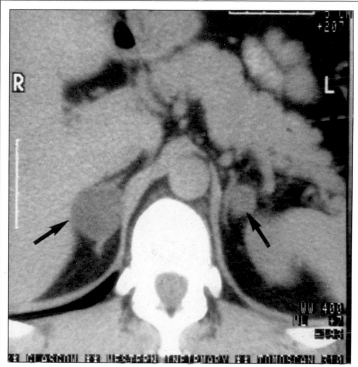

Figure 9

Figure 10 Adrenal venography in the same patient as Figure 9 showing the adenoma in the right adrenal but failing to show the smaller lesion on the left. Venography is now less often required for localization. Considerable expertise is necessary for adequate visualization of the adrenal circulation. There is a risk of adrenal infarction, especially if there has been extravasation of contrast during the procedure

Figure 11 Adrenal tumors from the same patient as in Figures 9 and 10 after surgery. Analysis of tumor steroid content demonstrated a high concentration of aldosterone on the left only

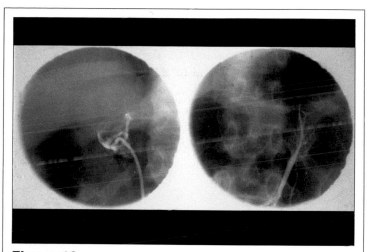

Figure 10

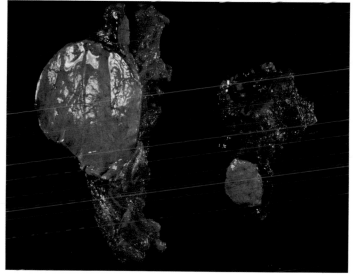

Figure 11

Figure 12 [75]Seleno-cholesterol scintigraphy may localize functioning tumors of the adrenal cortex. Sensitivity is increased by prior suppression of endogenous ACTH with dexamethasone. This scan shows the same aldosteronoma above the right kidney viewed from the back. Scintigraphy tends to be less sensitive than computed tomography

Figure 13 Venogram showing a left adrenal adenoma in a patient with primary aldosteronism

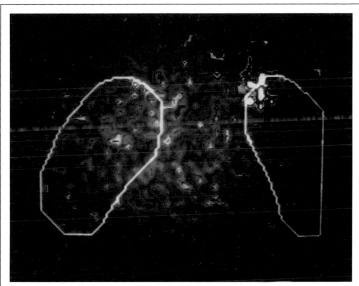

Figure 12

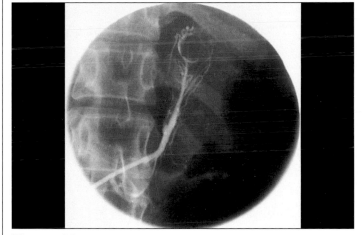

Figure 13

Figure 14 On the left is a typical aldosteronoma. On the right is an example of nodular hyperplasia of the adrenal cortex, which is present in idiopathic aldosteronism and, more commonly, in up to 20% of patients with primary hypertension

Figure 15 Axillary striae in a young man with pituitary-dependent Cushing's disease. The mechanism of hypertension in Cushing's syndrome is not entirely established. Hypokalemia is unusual unless there is ectopic secretion of ACTH, most often from a carcinoid tumor

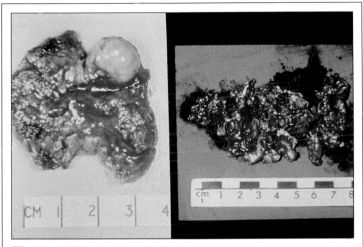

Figure 14

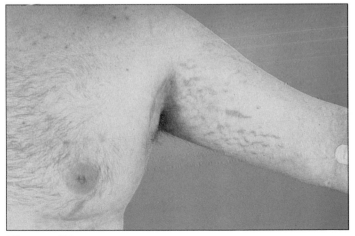

Figure 15

Figure 16 Ultrasonographic abdominal scan showing a solid left suprarenal mass above the kidney, which was an adrenal pheochromocytoma. Ultrasonography may fail to detect smaller lesions and computed tomography is more sensitive. In difficult cases, inferior vena caval sampling at different levels for measurements of catecholamines may be helpful

Figure 17 Ultrasonographic scan of the abdomen showing a large right adrenal pheochromocytoma containing several fluid-filled areas representing areas of necrosis

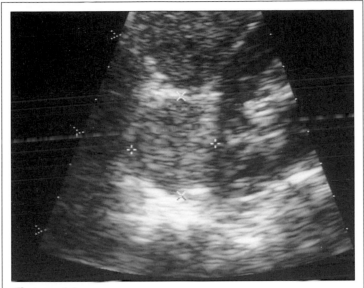

Figure 16

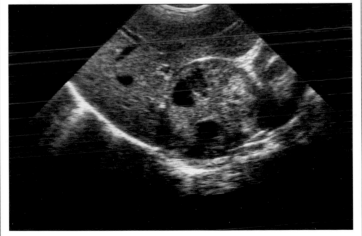

Figure 17

Figure 18 Typical appearance of the cut surface of an adrenal pheochromocytoma. The normal attenuated yellow gland can just be seen stretched over the rim. There are areas of cystic degeneration and hemorrhage. The patient had neurofibromatosis

Figure 19 Bilateral adrenal pheochromocytomas from a woman of 73 years who died with acute pulmonary edema caused by severe hypertension. There was also medullary carcinoma of the thyroid which established the diagnosis of multiple endocrine neoplasia type 2a, a condition that is inherited as a Mendelian dominant

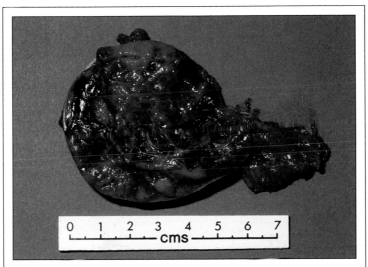

Figure 18

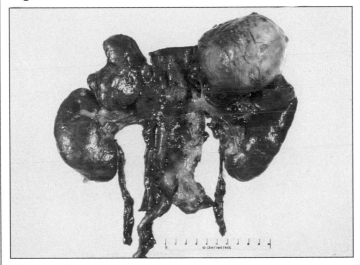

Figure 19

Figure 20 An electron micrograph showing the typical appearance of a collection of large pheochromocytoma cells. They are packed with dense 'neuroendocrine' granules of catecholamine type

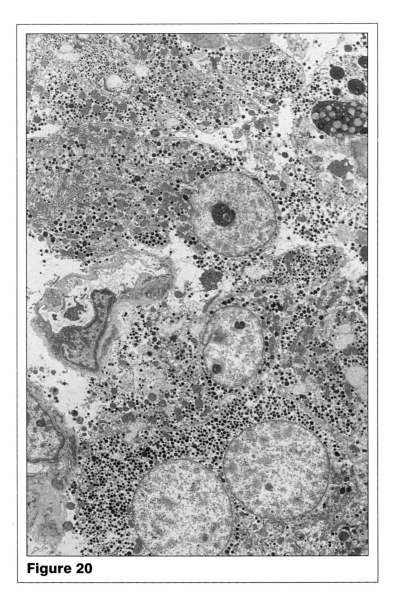

Figure 20

Figure 21 About 80% of pheochromocytomas take up [^{131}I]met-iodobenzylguanidine (MIBG). Scintigraphy after MIBG administration has here demonstrated a right adrenal pheochromocytoma viewed from the back. If the tumor takes up radionuclide then MIBG may be useful in detecting metastases and sometimes can be used in treatment (large doses)

Figure 22 Malignant pheochromocytomas often metastasize to bone. A scan with technetium-labelled methyl diphosphonate here shows secondary deposits in the skull, spine and first left rib

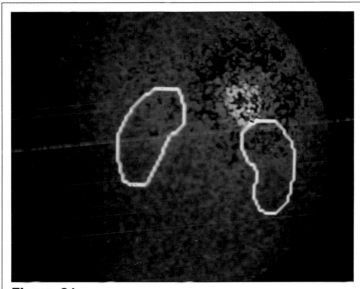

FIgure 21

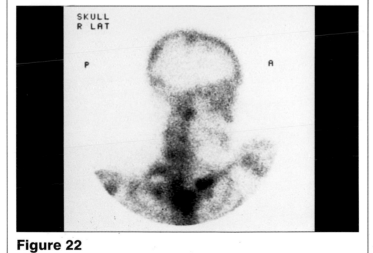

Figure 22

Figure 23 Hypertension also occurs in acromegaly, possibly due to an increase in body sodium content. Left ventricular hypertrophy may be greater than expected for the degree of hypertension

Figure 24 Typical appearances of the hands in acromegaly

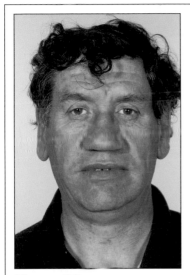

Figure 23

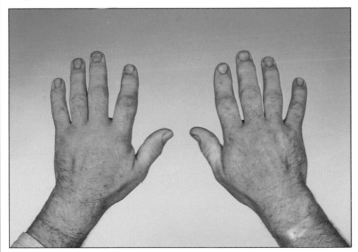

Figure 24

Figure 25 Intravenous urogram showing a ureteric calculus in the upper portion of the right ureter. There is an increased prevalence of hypertension in patients with primary hyperparathyroidism, but the mechanism is not well defined. In essential (primary) hypertension there is also an increased incidence of renal calculi

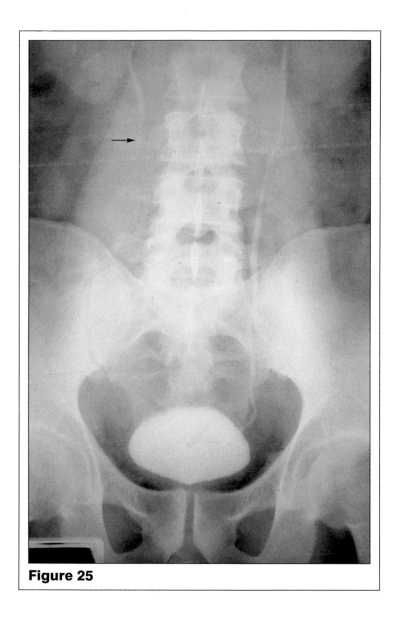

Figure 25

Figure 26 Continuous wave Doppler ultrasonography showing a normal wave form in the umbilical artery (above) and vein (below)

Figure 27 Continuous wave Doppler ultrasonography in a patient with severe pregnancy-associated hypertension, showing absent diastolic flow in the umbilical artery (above) and reduced flow in the vein (below). This flow pattern is commonly associated with marked growth retardation of the fetus. In pre-eclampsia, abnormal flow patterns may also be detected in the uterine arteries

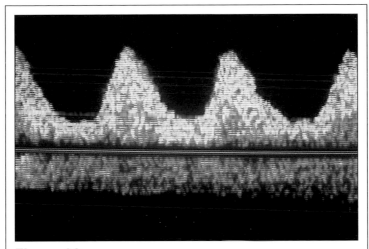

Figure 26

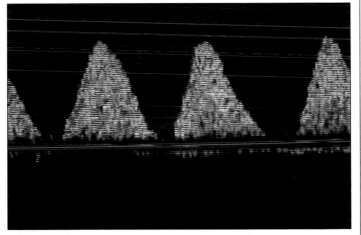

Figure 27

Figure 28 Part of the chest radiograph from a patient with coarctation of the aorta. Enlarged collateral vessels have caused marked notching of the lower margins of the ribs and the aortic knuckle is reduced. Coarctation is a very rare cause of hypertension but is quite common in Turner's syndrome (gonadal dysgenesis due to 45,X karyotype)

Figure 29 Digital subtraction angiogram from a 14-year-old girl with hypertension and diminished femoral pulses. There is a coarctation just distal to the left subclavian artery. A greatly enlarged internal mammary artery (to the left) is providing collateral flow

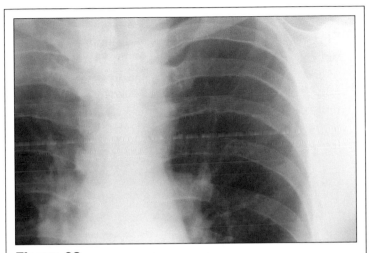

Figure 28

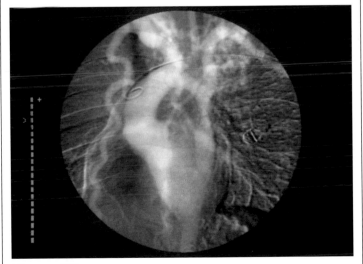

Figure 29

Figure 30 A thoracic aorta at autopsy. There is a tight coarctation in the center just above the origin of the row of intercostal arteries. Note the early atheroma above but not below the coarctation. The patient was a male of 20 years who died of an aortic dissection and had marked left ventricular hypertrophy

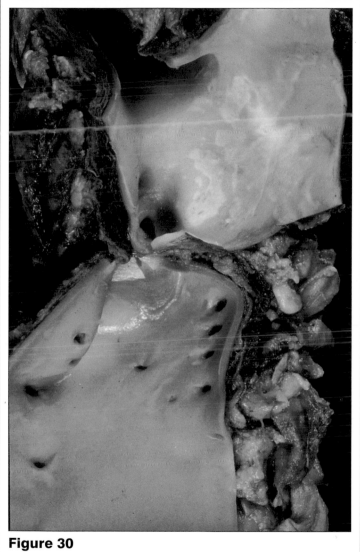

Figure 30

Figure 31 The development of a corneal arcus before 60 years of age signifies hypercholesterolemia and is associated with a high risk of coronary heart disease

Figure 32 Histology of a fatty streak in the intima of the human aorta. The raised area comprises lipid-rich 'foam cells' derived from smooth muscle cells which have migrated from the media and from macrophages which originate as blood monocytes. Fat is stained red with oil red O

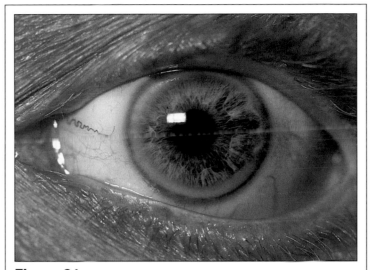

Figure 31

Figure 32

Figure 33 A human renal glomerulus from a patient with long-standing diabetes mellitus showing several stages in the formation of Kimmelstiel–Wilson nodules in the mesangium of several lobules

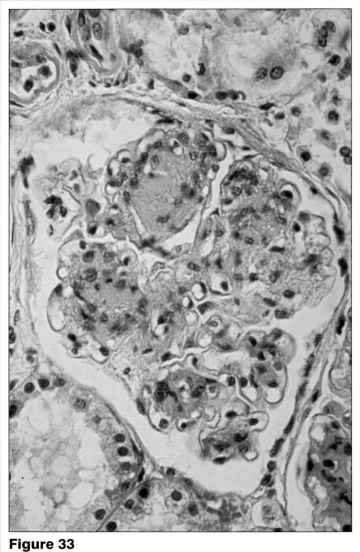

Figure 33

Figure 34 An electron micrograph from a patient with diabetic microvascular disease showing an arteriole. The smooth muscle cells of the media are largely replaced by homogeneous deposits of material which resemble basement membrane, probably deriving both from synthesis of excess basement membrane material and accumulation of proteins from the plasma

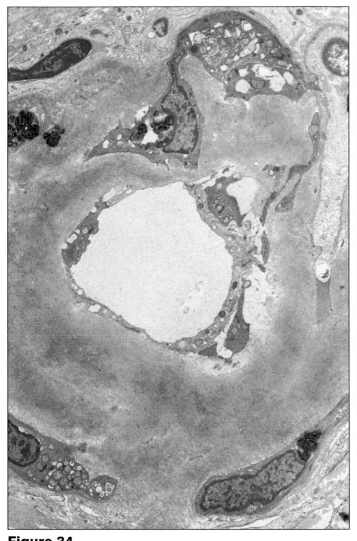

Figure 34

Figure 35 An electron micrograph showing a glomerular capillary wall in diabetes mellitus. There is gross thickening of the basement membrane represented as a homogeneous band. There is also fusion of the foot processes of the podocyte

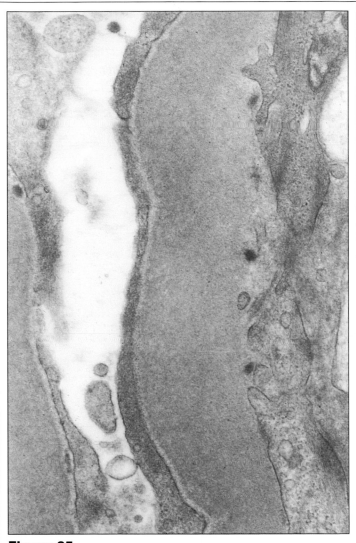

Figure 35

Acknowledgements

Drs Patricia Morley, Andrew Morris, Henry Dargie, James McLenachan, Jehoida Brown, John Connell, Andrew Collier, John Kingdom, Ian More, Amir Azmy and Mr Gerard Hillen all contributed slides and the authors thank them.

Selected bibliography

Pheochromocytoma
Bravo, E. L. and Gifford, R. W. (1984). Phaeochromo-cytoma: diagnosis, localization and management. *N. Engl. J. Med.*, **311**, 1298–303

Miscellaneous
Primary hyperparathyroidism
Dominiczak, A. F., Lyall, F., Morton, J. J., Dargie, H. J., Boyle, I. T., Tune, T. T., Murray, G. and Semple, P. F. (1990). Blood pressure, left ventricular mass and intracellular calcium in primary hyperparathyroidism. *Clin. Sci.*, 78, 127–32

Acromegaly
Davies, D. L., Beastall, G., Connell, J. M. C., Fraser, R., McCruden, D. and Teasdale, G. M. (1985). Body composition, blood pressure and the renin angiotensin system in acromegaly. *J. Hypertension*, **3** (Suppl. 3), S413–15

Gestational hypertension
Redman, C. W. G. (1990). Platelets and the beginnings of preeclampsia. *N. Engl. J. Med.*, **323**, 478–80

Jacobson, S. L., Imhof, R., Manning, N. *et al.* (1990). The value of Doppler assessment of the uteroplacental circulation in predicting preeclampsia or intrauterine growth retardation. *Am. J. Obstet. Gynecol.*, **162**, 110–14

Coarctation of the aorta

Liberthson, R. R., Pennington, D. C., Jacobs, M. L. and Daggett, W. M. (1979). Coarctation of the aorta: review of 234 patients and clarification of management problems. *Am. J. Cardiol.*, **43**, 835–40

Other risk factors

Wilhelmson, L. (1988). Coronary heart disease: epidemiology of smoking and intervention studies of smoking. *Am. Heart J.*, **115**, 242–9

Dollery, C. T. and Brennan, P. J. (1988). The Medical Research Council Hypertension Trial: the smoking patient. *Am. Heart J.*, **115**, 276–81

Modan, M., Halkin, H., Almog, S., Lusky, A., Eshkolo, A., Shefi, A., Shitrit, A. and Fuchs, Z. (1985). Hyperinsulinaemia. A link between hypertension, obesity and glucose intolerance. *J. Clin. Invest.*, **75**, 809–17

Reaven, G. M. and Hoffman, B. B. (1989). Hypertension as a disease of carbohydrate and lipoprotein metabolism. *Am. J. Med.*, **87** (Suppl. 6A), 25–65

Carlsen, J. E., Køber, L., Torp-Peterson, C. and Johansen, P. (1990). Relation between dose of bendrofluazide, antihypertensive effect and adverse biochemical effects. *Br. Med. J.*, **300**, 975–8

Castelli, W. P. and Anderson, K. (1986). A population at risk. Prevalence of high cholesterol levels in hypertensive patients in the Framingham Study. *Am. J. Med.*, **80** (Suppl. 2A), 523–32

Thomson, G. R. (1989). *A Handbook of Hyperlipidaemia.* (London: Current Science)

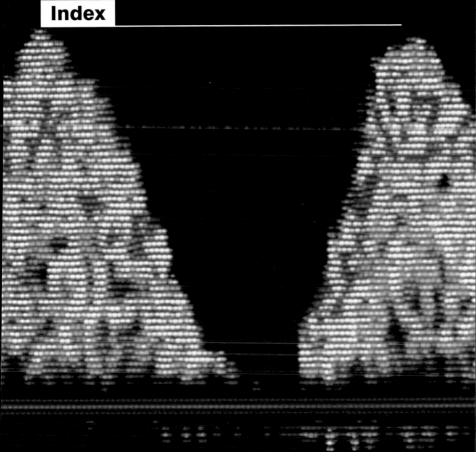

Index

Contents of Volume 1

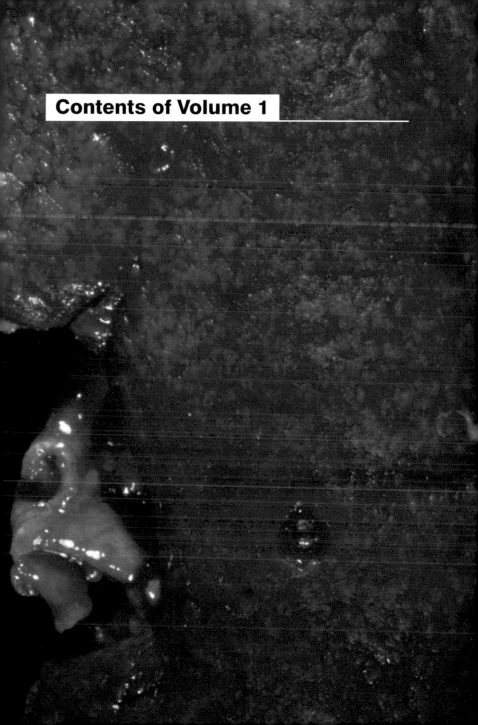

Contents of Volume 1

List of illustrations in Volume 1

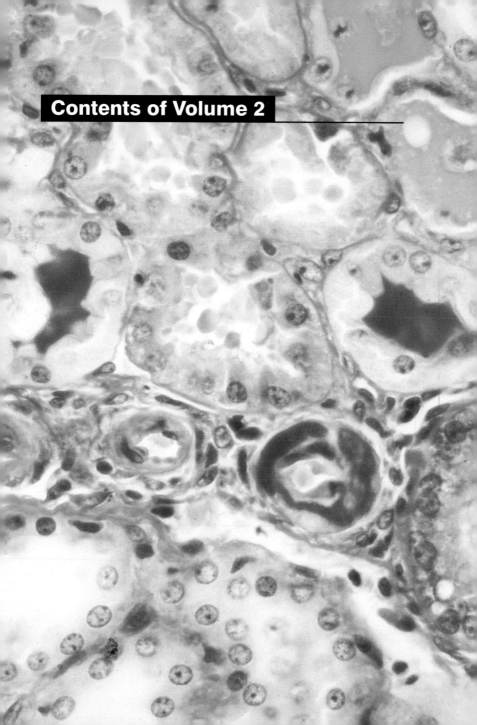

Contents of Volume 2

Contents of Volume 2

List of illustrations in Volume 2

Notes

Notes

Notes

Notes

Notes

Notes

ADALAT® CC
(nifedipine)
Extended Release Tablets
For Oral Use

PZ500005

DESCRIPTION

ADALAT® CC is an extended release tablet dosage form of the calcium channel blocker nifedipine. Nifedipine is 3,5-pyridinedicarboxylic acid, 1,4-dihydro-2,6-dimethyl-4-(2-nitrophenyl)-dimethyl ester, $C_{17}H_{18}N_2O_6$, and has the structural formula:

Nifedipine is a yellow crystalline substance, practically insoluble in water but soluble in ethanol. It has a molecular weight of 346.3. ADALAT CC tablets consist of an external coat and an internal core. Both contain nifedipine, the coat as a slow release formulation and the core as a fast release formulation. ADALAT CC tablets contain either 30, 60, or 90 mg of nifedipine for once-a-day oral administration.

Inert ingredients in the formulation are: hydroxypropylcellulose, lactose, corn starch, crospovidone, microcrystalline cellulose, silicon dioxide, and magnesium stearate. The inert ingredients in the film coating are: hydroxypropylmethylcellulose, polyethylene glycol, ferric oxide, and titanium dioxide.

CLINICAL PHARMACOLOGY

Nifedipine is a calcium ion influx inhibitor (slow-channel blocker or calcium ion antagonist) which inhibits the transmembrane influx of calcium ions into vascular smooth muscle and cardiac muscle. The contractile processes of vascular smooth muscle and cardiac muscle are dependent upon the movement of extracellular calcium ions into these cells through specific ion channels. Nifedipine selectively inhibits calcium ion influx across the cell membrane of vascular smooth muscle and cardiac muscle without altering serum calcium concentrations.

Mechanism of Action: The mechanism by which nifedipine reduces arterial blood pressure involves peripheral arterial vasodilatation and consequently, a reduction in peripheral vascular resistance. The increased peripheral vascular resistance is an underlying cause of hypertension results from an increase in active tension in the vascular smooth muscle. Studies have demonstrated that the increase in active tension reflects an increase in cytosolic free calcium.

Nifedipine is a peripheral arterial vasodilator which acts directly on vascular smooth muscle. The binding of nifedipine to voltage-dependent and possibly receptor-operated channels in vascular smooth muscle results in an inhibition of calcium influx through these channels. Stores of intracellular calcium in vascular smooth muscle are limited and thus dependent upon the influx of extracellular calcium for contraction to occur. The reduction in calcium influx by nifedipine causes arterial vasodilation and decreased peripheral vascular resistance which results in reduced arterial blood pressure.

Pharmacokinetics and Metabolism: Nifedipine is completely absorbed after oral administration. The bioavailability of nifedipine as ADALAT CC relative to immediate release nifedipine is in the range of 84%-89%. After ingestion of ADALAT CC tablets under fasting conditions, plasma concentrations peak at about 2.5-5 hours with a second small peak or shoulder evident at approximately 6-12 hours post dose. The elimination half-life of nifedipine administered as ADALAT CC is approximately 7 hours in contrast to the known 2 hour elimination half-life of nifedipine administered as an immediate release capsule.

When ADALAT CC is administered as multiples of 30 mg tablets over a dose range of 30 mg to 90 mg, the area under the curve (AUC) is dose proportional; however, the peak plasma concentration for the 90 mg dose given as 3×30 mg is 29% greater than predicted from the 30 mg and 60 mg doses.

Two 30 mg ADALAT CC tablets may be interchanged with a 60 mg ADALAT CC tablet. Three 30 mg ADALAT CC tablets, however, result in substantially higher C_{max} values than those after a single 90 mg ADALAT CC tablet. Three 30 mg tablets should, therefore, not be considered interchangeable with a 90 mg tablet.

Once daily dosing of ADALAT CC under fasting conditions results in decreased fluctuations in the plasma concentration of nifedipine when compared to t.i.d. dosing with immediate release nifedipine capsules. The mean peak plasma concentration of nifedipine following a 90 mg ADALAT CC tablet, administered under fasting conditions, is approximately 115 ng/mL. When ADALAT CC is given immediately after a high fat meal in healthy volunteers, there is an average increase of 60% in the peak plasma nifedipine concentration, a prolongation in the time to peak concentration, but no significant change in the AUC. Plasma concentrations of nifedipine when ADALAT CC is taken after a fatty meal result in slightly lower peaks compared to the same daily dose of the immediate release formulation administered in three divided doses. This may be, in part, because ADALAT CC is less bioavailable than the immediate release formulation.

Nifedipine is extensively metabolized to highly water soluble, inactive metabolites accounting for 60% to 80% of the dose excreted in the urine. Only traces (less than 0.1% of the dose) of the unchanged form can be detected in the urine. The remainder is excreted in the feces in metabolized form, most likely as a result of biliary excretion.

Notes